GINGER & TURMERIC

THE GOODNESS OF
GINGER &
TURMERIC

40 FLAVOURSOME ANTI-INFLAMMATORY RECIPES

EMILY JONZEN
PHOTOGRAPHY BY FAITH MASON

KYLE BOOKS

CONTENTS

SPICE SENSATIONS

Ginger and turmeric sometimes take the form of an unloved jar in a spice rack or a shrivelled root in the bottom of a vegetable drawer, yet these wonderful ingredients have the power to enliven a wealth of dishes beyond curries and stir-fries, as well as providing myriad of potential health benefits.

Both ginger and turmeric are tropical perennial plants belonging to the Zingiberaceae family and are native to Southern Asia. The roots, or rhizomes, are harvested and sold either fresh, dried or ground in a spice form. Ginger is renowned for its vibrant, citrusy flavour and fiery kick, whilst turmeric is earthy, mildly citrusy and slightly sweet. Their distinctive flavours, and the particularly vibrant colour of turmeric, have seen these roots become part of the foundation of Asian, Indian, Middle Eastern and West Indian cooking, but their uses extend far beyond the kitchen.

THE GOODNESS OF GINGER & TURMERIC

Ginger and turmeric have had important roles to play in traditional remedies for many centuries. In Ayurvedic medicine, ginger serves as – among things – a digestion aid and anti-inflammatory agent, whilst turmeric has long been used to heal wounds. Although there may be an element of folklore in the ancient uses of ginger and turmeric, numerous recent scientific studies have suggested that they contain significant health benefits:

♦ Both contain powerful anti-inflammatory and antioxidant properties, which some clinical trials have shown to decrease the risk of obesity, diabetes and heart disease, as well as joint and digestive ailments.
♦ Ginger has been proven to help with gastrointestinal ailments and morning sickness in pregnant women.
♦ Turmeric is heralded for its antifungal and antibacterial properties.
♦ The curcumin compound in turmeric is particularly anti-inflammatory, and studies have shown that pairing it with black pepper can help enhance its absorption into the bloodstream.

A note on preserving

The process of preserving, fermenting and pickling produces gut-friendly bacteria, meaning it can make ginger and turmeric even better for you. The bacteria produced breaks down the cellulose found in some foods, making them easier to digest.

When preparing raw ingredients for fermenting (such as sauerkraut), make sure that all of the surfaces and utensils you use are scrupulously clean.

As with all preserving, it is imperative that pickles and ferments are stored in sterilised jars to preserve freshness and prevent the growth of bacteria.

To sterilise jars and bottles, heat the oven to 140°C/120°C fan/ gas mark 1. Wash the jars and bottles in hot, soapy water and rinse well. Place on a baking tray and put them in the oven for 10 minutes, until hot and dry. If using kilner jars, remove the rubber seals and place them in boiling water for 10 minutes to avoid damage from the oven.

Spoon or pour the foods you are pickling or fermenting into the jars while they still are hot and seal immediately to preserve the freshness. Store in a cool, dry place and refrigerate after opening.

BUYING, STORING AND PREPARING

Ginger and turmeric are available either dried or fresh, and both have benefits for different recipes. With correct storage they can last for a decent amount of time.

Dried

Dried ginger and turmeric have been widely used for generations and are readily available in all supermarkets.

Once opened, the spices can be stored in a cool, dark place for up to a year. They will still be edible when older than this, but over time their flavour and pungency will decrease and they will have a slightly dusty taste.

Dried and ground spices have a higher concentration in flavour than fresh, and are more commonly used in curries, dry spice mixes and baking. A quarter of a teaspoon of the dried spices can be substituted for one tablespoon of freshly grated root in most recipes, but it is best to use dried spices in baking, so as not to affect the moisture content.

Fresh

When buying fresh roots, look for ones with smooth, taut skin without wrinkles and with a delicately spicy aroma.

To store, wrap the roots in kitchen or greaseproof paper and leave in the fridge, where they will keep for up to two weeks. Alternatively, freeze the peeled roots for up to three months, and grate them into dishes directly from the freezer.

Matchsticks and fine slivers can add beauty and vibrancy, as well as distinctive flavours, to the presentation of dishes. Cooking fresh ginger and turmeric will mellow out their flavours and lend an aroma to your cooking, but you can also enjoy them raw, as a garnish, in salad dressings or drinks.

When using fresh roots, both ginger and turmeric need to be peeled. Their irregular shape means that using a vegetable peeler can result in taking off excess flesh, so the easiest way to remove the thin, delicate skin is by scraping it off using the edge of a teaspoon. You can then grate, chop, slice or cut the roots into matchsticks, depending on the recipe.

Golden turmeric

Turmeric provides a wonderful colour, but its stubborn vibrancy may be off-putting for those not used to it. The lurid yellow will cling to hands and any surface it touches, but do not despair: a good scrub with soap will remove any stains, and surfaces and chopping boards will be as good as new if rubbed with a squeeze of lemon. For particularly stubborn stains, try sprinkling it with a little bicarbonate of soda and a few drops of water, which will draw the stain out without chemicals.

LIGHT
BITES

CARAWAY ROASTED ROOTS

*VEGETARIAN *DAIRY-FREE *GLUTEN-FREE

The earthy anise flavour of caraway is the perfect companion to sweet, roasted root vegetables. Try serving this as a side to roast chicken or pork, or with a simple salad.

Serves 4 as a side, or 2 as a main course with salad

4 whole raw beetroot, scrubbed and cut into wedges
1 tablespoon olive oil
1 teaspoon caraway seeds
1 teaspoon ground turmeric
Pinch of chilli flakes
2 teaspoons runny honey
2 teaspoons balsamic vinegar
Salt and freshly ground black pepper
300g baby carrots (use heritage when in season), scrubbed and cut in half
A handful of chopped parsley, to serve

1. Preheat the oven to 220°C/200°C fan/gas mark 8.

2. Tip the beetroot into a roasting tin and pour over the olive oil. Stir to coat the wedges in the oil, then roast in the oven for 20 minutes.

3. In a small bowl, mix together the caraway seeds, turmeric, chilli flakes, honey, balsamic vinegar and some salt and pepper.

4. Add the carrots to the roasting tin, pour over this dressing and give everything a good mix until the carrots and beetroot are well coated. Return to the oven for a further 20–25 minutes, until the vegetables are just tender.

5. Scatter with the chopped parsley to serve.

PERSIAN HERB OMELETTE *VEGETARIAN

This twist on the traditional Kuku Sabzi is a delicious and aromatic alternative to a European-style omelette. The additions of flour and baking powder give a firm but light structure to the omelette, making it easy to cut into wedges. It's equally delicious straight out of the oven or eaten cold.

Serves 4

1 tablespoon olive oil
1 leek, white and green parts, finely sliced
8 medium eggs
2 spring onions, finely sliced
Handful each of parsley, dill, coriander and chives, finely chopped
1 tablespoon plain flour
1 teaspoon baking powder
2 teaspoons ground turmeric
Salt and freshly ground black pepper
Squeeze of lemon juice
75g feta, crumbled
Green salad, to serve (optional)

1. Preheat the oven to 200°C/180°C fan/gas mark 6.

2. Heat the oil in a large, ovenproof frying pan and add the leeks. Fry for 6–8 minutes over a low-medium heat, stirring from time to time, until softened.

3. Meanwhile, beat the eggs in a large bowl and add the spring onions, herbs, flour, baking powder and turmeric. Season well and pour the egg mixture into the pan, giving it an initial stir to combine with the leeks. Cook over a low heat for 10 minutes, then continue cooking in the oven for a further 5 minutes, until just set.

4. Allow the omelette to stand for 5 minutes before cutting into wedges. Squeeze over some lemon juice and scatter over the crumbled feta. Serve with a green salad, if you wish.

Try serving this with the Carrot & Fennel Salad on page 22.

GINGER & KIMCHI FRIED RICE

*VEGETARIAN *DAIRY-FREE *GLUTEN-FREE

This simple, quick stir-fry makes great use of sour and fiery kimchi and is an easy introduction to Korean cooking. Not only does kimchi taste delicious, but it is also full of healthy, gut-friendly bacteria. Sweet and spicy gochujang paste, made from red chillies, balances out the sourness of the kimchi.

Serves 4

3 teaspoons sunflower oil
2–3cm piece of ginger, peeled and finely grated
2 garlic cloves, crushed
2 carrots, peeled and roughly diced
4 spring onions, sliced
225g kimchi, drained and chopped
700g steamed rice
4–5 tablespoons kimchi juice from the jar
1–2 tablespoons gochujang paste
4 free-range eggs
2 sheets of seaweed, such as nori or gim, shredded
2 teaspoons toasted sesame seeds

1. Heat 2 teaspoons of the oil in a large frying pan or wok. Add the ginger, garlic and carrot and stir-fry for 1–2 minutes, until fragrant and beginning to soften. Add half of the spring onions to the pan along with the kimchi and continue to stir-fry for a further minute.

2. Tip the rice into the pan and fry for 1–2 minutes, to allow the rice to crispen up slightly, before adding the kimchi juice and gochujang paste to the pan. Stir for 1–2 minutes, until the rice is piping hot.

3. Meanwhile, heat the remaining oil in a separate pan and fry the eggs to your liking.

4. Serve the rice topped with a fried egg, the remainder of the spring onions and a sprinkling of shredded seaweed and sesame seeds.

Gochujang paste is available in large supermarkets, but if you can't find it, sriracha would also work well.

GOLDEN SWEETCORN SOUP

This sunny, golden soup is deliciously creamy and can be ready in less than 40 minutes. It is wonderful on its own but the salty kick of the pancetta and slight sharpness of the goats' cheese transform the soup into something that would make a wonderful weekend lunch or starter for entertaining.

Serves 4

2 teaspoons olive oil
1 medium onion, diced
2 garlic cloves, crushed
1 tablespoon ground turmeric
200g potato, such as King
   Edwards, peeled and diced
Sprig of thyme
500g sweetcorn kernels
   (frozen or tinned, drained
   weight)
1 litre good-quality chicken or
   vegetable stock
4 slices of pancetta
4 slices of baguette
Salt and freshly ground black
   pepper
100g soft goats' cheese
Pinch of chilli flakes, to serve

1. Heat the oil in a large saucepan and add the onion. Cook over a low-medium heat for 8–10 minutes, until translucent. Add the garlic and turmeric and fry for a minute, until fragrant.

2. Stir in the diced potato, along with the thyme and sweetcorn kernels. Cover with the stock and bring to the boil. Reduce to a simmer and cook for 20–25 minutes, until the vegetables are tender. Discard the thyme.

3. Whilst the soup is cooking, preheat the grill to medium. Grill the pancetta, alongside the baguette slices, for 1–2 minutes each side, until crisp and golden. Set aside.

4. Allow the soup to cool a little before blitzing with a stick blender until smooth, reheat if necessary and season to taste.

5. To serve, spread the baguette slices with the goats' cheese and float on the soup or serve alongside. Crumble the pancetta over the soup and sprinkle lightly with chilli flakes.

CARROT & FENNEL SALAD *VEGETARIAN *DAIRY-FREE *GLUTEN-FREE

This light and crunchy salad is ideal for a summertime lunch. Serve on its own or alongside grilled chicken or fish.

Serves 4

2 large carrots, peeled and coarsely grated or shredded using a julienne peeler
1 large fennel bulb, finely sliced, preferably using a mandoline
A handful of cashew nuts, roughly chopped
A handful of chives, finely chopped

For the dressing
Juice of ½ orange
1 teaspoon white wine vinegar
2–3cm piece of ginger, peeled and finely grated
1 tablespoon fruity olive oil
Salt and freshly ground black pepper

1. Toss the carrot and fennel together with the cashews and chives.

2. Whisk together the orange juice, vinegar, ginger and olive oil and season with salt and pepper. Pour the dressing over the salad, toss together and serve.

GINGER CHICKEN BROTH *DAIRY-FREE

Infinitely soothing and heralded for its medicinal properties for generations, homemade chicken soup is the ultimate in health-giving comfort food. The addition of ginger bolsters the nutritional benefits, as well as adding a spicy depth to this delicate broth.

Serves 4–6

4 banana (echalion) shallots, cut in half
6 garlic cloves, lightly crushed with the back of a knife
1 medium carrot, scrubbed and cut into large chunks
2 stalks of celery, cut in half
200g ginger, peeled and thickly sliced
8 black peppercorns
1 whole chicken, jointed into 8 pieces, or 4 whole chicken legs and two drumsticks

To finish
150g shiitake mushrooms, sliced
Soy sauce, to taste
4 spring onions, finely sliced
1 red chilli, finely sliced
A handful of coriander leaves, roughly chopped

1. Put the shallots, garlic, carrot, celery, ginger and peppercorns in a large pan or casserole dish. Add the chicken pieces and pour over 3½–4 litres of water – enough to completely cover all the ingredients. Place the pan over a medium–high heat and bring to the boil. As soon as it reaches boiling point, reduce the heat to a gentle simmer and leave the broth to bubble away, skimming the scum from the surface from time to time, for 30 minutes.

2. If you are using a jointed whole chicken, remove the breasts from the pan and set aside in the fridge until needed. Continue to gently simmer the broth for 2½ hours, until the meat is tender and the broth has a rich flavour.

3. Strain the broth into another pan and simmer for 10–15 minutes, until reduced slightly. Discard the vegetables and shred the meat (including the breast, if using). Return the shredded meat to the pan, add the shiitake mushrooms and simmer for 5 minutes. Season with soy sauce and ladle into bowls, topped with the spring onions, chilli and coriander.

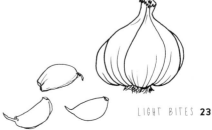

CANNELLINI & CHORIZO HASH *GLUTEN-FREE

This fortifying brunch is just the thing if you're feeling slightly delicate. The combination of protein from the beans and eggs, fat from the chorizo and the powerful antioxidant and anti-inflammatory properties of turmeric will help soothe you back to normality.

Serves 4

120g diced chorizo
2 teaspoons olive oil
1 teaspoon smoked paprika
2 x 400g tins cannellini beans, drained and patted dry
1 garlic clove, crushed
4 spring onions, sliced
4 free-range eggs
1 teaspoon ground turmeric
1 teaspoon sesame seeds, toasted
Squeeze of lemon juice

1. Tip the chorizo into a large, non-stick frying pan and place over a low-medium heat. Fry the chorizo for 4–5 minutes, until crisp and golden. Remove the chorizo with a slotted spoon and drain on kitchen paper, leaving the oil behind in the pan.

2. Add 1 teaspoon of the olive oil and the paprika to the pan, increase the heat then add the beans, crushing lightly with the back of a spatula. Fry for 2–3 minutes, stirring occasionally, until the beans have crisped slightly. Stir in the garlic and half of the spring onions and continue to fry for 1–2 minutes, stirring from time to time. Lower the heat, return the chorizo to the pan and keep warm.

3. Heat the remaining teaspoon of oil in a separate frying pan and once very hot, fry the eggs for 2 minutes, until the whites have just set. Sprinkle over the turmeric and sesame seeds and serve immediately on top of the beans, with a squeeze of lemon juice and the remaining spring onions.

It may seem counter-intuitive, but adding the chorizo to a cold pan will help to render more fat and make it all the more crisp.

TOMATO, GINGER & RED ONION SALAD

*VEGETARIAN *DAIRY-FREE *GLUTEN-FREE

This robust salad makes a great side to a fiery curry, and also goes well with grilled meat or fish and a dollop of yogurt. It's also just as good served on its own.

Serves 4 – 6

1 teaspoon nigella (black onion) seeds
1 red onion, very finely sliced
Juice of 1 lemon
Salt
2 teaspoons rapeseed oil
2–3cm piece of ginger, peeled and finely grated
6 large vine tomatoes, roughly chopped
A small handful of coriander, roughly chopped

1. Toast the nigella seeds in a small frying pan for 1 minute, until fragrant. Remove from the pan and set aside.

2. Tip the onion and lemon juice into a bowl, sprinkle with salt to taste and leave to soften for 10 minutes.

3. Stir in the remaining ingredients and serve immediately, sprinkled with the nigella seeds.

MAINS

LENTILS, HALLOUMI & COURGETTES

*VEGETARIAN *GLUTEN-FREE

Marinating salty and savoury halloumi elevates it to another level of flavour. Teamed with delicate courgette and earthy lentils, this summery, comforting dish shows that meat-free cooking need not mean compromising on flavour.

Serves 4

400g courgettes, cut into
  1cm-thick slices
1 pack of halloumi (250g),
  cut into 1cm-thick slices
Zest and juice of 1 lemon
50ml good-quality olive oil
2–3cm piece of turmeric,
  peeled and finely grated
2 garlic cloves, crushed
A handful of chives, chopped
A handful of mint, finely
  chopped
Pinch of chilli flakes
Freshly ground black pepper
1 good-quality vegetable
  stock cube
200g uncooked Puy lentils
120ml natural yogurt (low-fat
  or fat-free, if liked)
A small handful each of
  chopped chives and mint
  leaves, to serve

1. Tip the courgettes and halloumi into a bowl and add the lemon zest and juice, olive oil, turmeric, garlic, half of the herbs, and the chilli flakes. Season with a good grind of black pepper. Stir gently so as not to break up the halloumi and set aside to marinate for 20 minutes.

2. Meanwhile, pour 1.5 litres of boiling water into a pan, stir in the stock cube and tip in the lentils. Simmer for 20–25 minutes, until just tender. Drain, set aside and keep warm.

3. Heat a non-stick frying pan until smoking hot. Lift the halloumi and courgettes out of the marinade with a slotted spoon and blot on kitchen paper to remove most of the moisture. Add the halloumi and courgettes in a single layer and fry for 2 minutes on each side, until golden. You will probably need to do this in two batches.

4. Pour the yogurt into the remaining marinade and mix to combine. Stir through the lentils and serve, topped with the courgettes, halloumi and remaining herbs.

TURMERIC & PANEER CURRY

A vegetarian spin on Jalfrezi, this dish uses paneer – a delicate yet firm Indian cheese that mellows out the rich spice.

Serves 4

1½ tablespoons vegetable oil
1½ teaspoons cumin seeds
5cm piece of ginger, peeled and finely grated
1 large onion (or 2 small), finely sliced
2 garlic cloves, crushed
1 teaspoon hot chilli powder
1 teaspoon ground coriander
1½ teaspoons ground turmeric
Salt and freshly ground black pepper
1 red pepper, cored, deseeded and finely sliced
1 green pepper, cored, deseeded and finely sliced
2 large, very ripe tomatoes, such as beef, cut into eighths
250g paneer, cut into 2cm cubes
Juice of ½ lemon
1–2 green chillies, sliced (optional)
A small handful of coriander leaves (optional)
Steamed rice or chapatis, to serve

1. Heat the oil in a large frying pan over a medium heat. Add the cumin seeds and half of the ginger and fry for 30 seconds, until fragrant. Tip in the onion and cook, stirring regularly, for 5–6 minutes, until softened but with a slight bite.

2. Add the garlic, cook for 1 minute, then add the chilli powder, ground coriander, turmeric and a pinch of salt and pepper. Give the spices a good stir before adding the peppers. Fry everything for a further 5 minutes, until the peppers have softened slightly.

3. Stir the tomatoes into the pan, along with 100ml water, and cook for a couple of minutes. Add the paneer, lower the heat and allow the mixture to bubble for 2–3 minutes, stirring occasionally, until the paneer is hot and covered with the sauce.

4. Sprinkle over the lemon juice, remaining ginger, chillies and coriander leaves (if using) and serve immediately with rice or chapatis.

BLACK BEAN TACOS & MANGO SALSA

*VEGETARIAN

These delicious tacos are filled with lightly spiced, smoky beans and topped with a vibrant mango salsa. Easy to make and ideal for entertaining or for a healthy, mid-week meal.

Serves 4

For the beans
2 teaspoons olive oil
1 red onion, finely chopped
2 garlic cloves, crushed
2 teaspoons ground cumin
1½ teaspoons ground turmeric
2 teaspoons smoked paprika
½–1 teaspoon chilli flakes
400g tin chopped tomatoes
2 tablespoons tomato purée
200ml vegetable stock
2 x 400g tins black beans, drained and rinsed
2 teaspoons honey, to taste

For the salsa
1 banana (echalion) shallot, finely diced
1 avocado, flesh roughly diced
1 medium, ripe mango, peeled and diced
1 red chilli, finely chopped
Juice of 2 limes
1 handful of coriander leaves, roughly chopped
Pinch of salt

To serve
12–16 ready-made soft tacos
150ml sour cream

1. To prepare the beans, heat the oil in a large pan and add the onion. Fry gently for 6–8 minutes, until softened. Add the garlic to the pan and fry for a further minute before adding the cumin, turmeric, smoked paprika and chilli flakes. Allow the spices to toast, stirring frequently, for a minute.

2. Add the chopped tomatoes, tomato purée, stock and black beans to the pan and bring to the boil. Lower the heat to a simmer and cook, stirring occasionally, for 20 minutes or so, until thickened. Add the honey to taste.

3. To make the salsa, stir all the ingredients together in a bowl. Set aside whilst the beans cook.

4. Heat a griddle pan or non-stick frying pan and lightly toast the tacos to warm through. Serve with spoonfuls of the bean mixture, salsa and sour cream or crème fraîche.

Serve the black beans and salsa with brown rice for a vegetarian chilli.

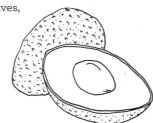

SPICED AUBERGINE & CAULI WITH LABNEH

*VEGETARIAN *GLUTEN-FREE

Ideal for vegetarian entertaining or for a simple, meat-free meal, the mix of fragrant vegetables, sweet and sharp pomegranates and creamy labneh will have you making this dish time and time again. It is easy to make your own labneh, or it is available in large supermarkets or Middle Eastern stores. You could also substitute it with a good-quality Greek-style yogurt.

Serves 4

For the labneh
500g good-quality strained
   Greek yogurt
1 teaspoon flakey sea salt

For the vegetables
300g baby aubergines, cut in
   half lengthways
1 head of cauliflower, cut into
   bite-sized florets
4 garlic cloves, crushed
Salt and freshly ground black
   pepper
2 tablespoons olive oil
1 teaspoon cumin seeds
1 tablespoon ras el hanout
   spice mix (available in most
   supermarkets)
2 teaspoons ground turmeric

cont. overleaf

1. Make the labneh the day before serving. Line a large sieve with a cheesecloth and suspend it over a bowl. Stir the salt into the yogurt, then spoon into the cheesecloth and tie the material into a tight bundle. Transfer to the fridge and leave to drain for 24 hours, until spreadable.

2. The next day, preheat the oven to 240°C/220°C fan/gas mark 9.

3. Put the aubergines, cauliflower and garlic into a large mixing bowl and season well with salt and pepper. Pour over the olive oil and add the cumin seeds, ras el hanout and turmeric. Give the mixture a good stir to coat the vegetables in the spice mix.

4. Scrape the vegetables into a large roasting tin and transfer to the oven. Roast for 20–25 minutes, turning halfway through cooking, until the vegetables are golden and just tender.

cont. overleaf

For the salad

1 red onion, finely sliced

Juice of 1 lemon

1 pomegranate, deseeded

A large handful each of parsley, mint and dill leaves, roughly chopped

2 teaspoons extra virgin olive oil

1 teaspoon pomegranate molasses

¼ teaspoon ground sumac

5. Whilst the vegetables are cooking, assemble the salad by tipping the onion into a salad bowl and pouring over the lemon juice. Set aside for 10 minutes to allow the onion to soften before adding the pomegranate and herbs.

6. Whisk together the olive oil, pomegranate molasses and sumac and pour over the salad just before serving.

7. To assemble, spoon the labneh onto a serving dish and spread it out using the back of a spoon. Tip the vegetables onto the labneh and serve with the salad.

VIETNAMESE PORK MEATBALLS

*DAIRY-FREE

These delicately spiced and flavoursome meatballs make a delicious, summery meal with soft noodles and sharp, pickled vegetables. Don't be put off by the long list of ingredients; this dish is so easy to prepare and both the meatballs and dipping sauce can be made up to 24 hours in advance and refrigerated until ready to cook.

Serves 4

For the meatballs
500g free-range pork mince
2 garlic cloves, crushed
2 shallots, finely chopped
5cm piece of ginger, peeled and finely grated
2–3cm piece of turmeric, peeled and finely grated
2 stalks of lemongrass, tough outer leaves removed, white part finely chopped
1 red chilli, finely chopped
2 teaspoons fish sauce
1–2 teaspoons groundnut oil

For the dipping sauce and vegetables
50ml fish sauce
50ml rice wine vinegar
Juice of 2 large limes
3 teaspoons palm sugar, ground with a pestle and mortar, or soft light brown sugar

cont. overleaf

1. To make the meatballs, put the pork mince into a bowl with the garlic, shallots, ginger, turmeric, lemongrass, chilli and fish sauce and mix together until well combined. Form the mixture into flattish, tablespoon-sized meatballs and set aside in the fridge. To get ahead, this can be done up to 24 hours in advance.

2. To prepare the vegetables and dipping sauce, combine the fish sauce, rice wine vinegar, lime juice and sugar and give it a taste – it should have a nice balance of saltiness, sourness and sweetness. Adjust the seasoning to taste.

cont. overleaf

2 medium carrots, peeled and
roughly grated
1 daikon or 250g radishes,
julienned or roughly grated

To serve
200g pack of rice vermicelli
noodles, cooked to packet
instructions, rinsed under
cold water and drained
½ head of round lettuce,
shredded
A handful each of coriander
and mint leaves, roughly
chopped
Lime wedges
1 red chilli, deseeded and
sliced

3. Put the grated carrots and
daikon/radish in a bowl and
pour over half the sauce. Toss
the vegetables in the sauce and
set aside to lightly pickle whilst
you cook the meatballs. Pour
the remainder of the sauce into
a small bowl and set aside for
dipping.

4. Heat the groundnut oil in
a non-stick frying pan and fry
the meatballs for 3–4 minutes
each side, until golden and
completely cooked through.

5. Serve the meatballs
and vegetables on a pile of
vermicelli, garnished with
lettuce, herbs, wedges of lime
and a sprinkling of chilli. Serve
the dipping sauce separately in
individual bowls.

GINGER BEER SHORT RIBS

A great source of iron, selenium and vitamin B12, beef short ribs are an indulgent yet nutritious meal. These unctuous ribs are spiked with fiery ginger beer and teamed with a crunchy and slightly sharp slaw.

Serves 4

2 teaspoons sunflower oil
2kg beef short ribs
Salt and freshly ground black pepper
500ml good-quality, ginger beer (see page 59)
1 large onion, sliced
4 garlic cloves, crushed
10cm piece of ginger, peeled and finely grated
250ml beef stock
1 star anise
2 teaspoons soy sauce
2 teaspoons Worcestershire sauce
2 sprigs of thyme

For the slaw
1 crisp red apple, cored and coarsely grated
2 medium carrots, peeled and coarsely grated
½ red cabbage, quartered, cored and shredded
4 spring onions, finely sliced
150ml buttermilk
1 teaspoon cider vinegar
Pinch of unrefined sugar
A handful of finely chopped chives

1. Preheat the oven to 170°C/ 150° C fan/gas mark 3.

2. Heat 1 teaspoon of oil in a large frying pan. Season the ribs with a little salt and pepper and add to the pan. Fry on all sides for 4–5 minutes. Once golden, transfer the ribs to a large casserole dish, deglaze the frying pan with a little of the ginger beer and add this to the dish with the ribs.

3. Wipe the pan clean and add the remaining 1 teaspoon of oil. Add the onion to the pan and fry for 3–4 minutes, until golden. Add the garlic and ginger and fry for a further minute, until fragrant. Scrape the onion mixture into the dish with the ribs and deglaze the frying pan with a little more of the ginger beer. Add this to the ribs, along with the remaining ginger beer, stock, star anise, soy sauce, Worcestershire sauce and thyme.

Bring the mixture to the boil, cover and transfer to the oven. Cook for 2–2½ hours, turning after 1 hour.

4. Meanwhile, combine the apple, carrot, cabbage and spring onions. Whisk together the buttermilk, cider vinegar, sugar and chives. Pour over the slaw and mix well. Season to taste.

5. When the beef is cooked (it should be falling off the bone), remove it from the pan and set aside to rest. Place the casserole over a high heat and reduce the sauce until fairly thick. Pour over the ribs.

6. Serve the short ribs, shredded if liked, alongside a generous serving of slaw. For an indulgent treat, serve the meat shredded with the slaw in a toasted brioche bun.

BEEF & GINGER STEW

This hearty stew with a hit of fiery ginger is ideal for slow, wintry cooking. Sweet and smoky hispi cabbage makes for a lively accompaniment.

Serves 4–6

800g good-quality stewing beef or shin, trimmed of any excess fat and sinew and cut into 2cm cubes
1 tablespoon plain flour, seasoned with sea salt and pepper
2 tablespoons olive oil
2 onions, sliced
2 stalks of celery, finely sliced
2 large carrots, peeled, cut in half and cut into 1–2cm thick slices
4 garlic cloves, crushed
10cm piece of ginger, peeled and roughly grated
1 tablespoon tomato purée
1 bay leaf
500ml good-quality beef stock
2 teaspoons Worcestershire sauce
1 whole hispi (sweetheart) cabbage, outer leaves removed, cut into 8 wedges
1 tablespoon butter, melted
A handful of roughly chopped parsley, to serve

1. Preheat the oven to 160°C/140°C fan/Gas Mark 3.

2. Toss the beef in the seasoned flour. Heat 1 tablespoon of the oil in a large casserole or ovenproof pan. Fry the meat in batches to brown on all sides, adding a little more oil as necessary between batches. Transfer the browned meat to a bowl and deglaze the pan with a little water, making sure to scrape the bottom of the pan as you go. Pour the deglazing juices over the browned meat and set aside.

3. Heat the remaining tablespoon of oil in the pan and fry the onions, celery and carrots until golden. Add the garlic, ginger and tomato purée to the pan and continue to fry for a further minute or two, until fragrant.

4. Return the meat and its juices to the pan and add the bay leaf, beef stock and Worcestershire sauce. Give everything a good stir, bring up to a simmer, cover with a lid and then transfer to the oven. Leave to cook for 2 hours, until the meat falls apart to the touch.

5. Lay the cabbage out on a board and brush all over with the melted butter. Heat a griddle pan until smoking hot and griddle the cabbage wedges for 3–4 minutes each side, until tender and charred. Serve with the stew, scattered with parsley.

MUSTARD, HERB & GINGER CHICKEN

Liven up roast chicken with a kick of ginger and mustard and a side of crisp hasselback potatoes.

Serves 4

4 stalks of celery, trimmed
1 whole free-range or organic chicken, about 1.5kg in weight
2 onions, cut in half
1 whole garlic bulb, cut in half horizontally
10cm piece of ginger, peeled, half bruised with a rolling pin, half finely grated
1 whole lemon, cut in half
4 sprigs of thyme, leaves removed from half
A small handful of parsley
1 tablespoon olive oil
30g butter, melted
800g new potatoes, washed
3 tablespoons whole-grain mustard
1 heaped tablespoon plain flour
250ml chicken stock
A head of butter lettuce, to serve (optional)
Salt and freshly ground black pepper

1. Preheat the oven to 200°C/180°C fan/Gas Mark 6.

2. Lay the celery out in a large roasting tin and pop the chicken on top. Place the onion halves around the chicken and then put half the garlic, the bruised ginger, half the lemon, 2 sprigs of thyme and all of the parsley inside the cavity of the chicken. Add the remaining lemon and garlic to the tin, ½ tablespoon of oil over the vegetables and brush the chicken skin with a little of the melted butter. Season with salt and pepper and transfer to the oven for 20 minutes.

3. Meanwhile, prepare the potatoes by making cuts across the width about 2mm apart and about two thirds of the way down each potato. Toss in the remaining ½ tablespoon of olive oil, season with salt and pepper and set aside.

4. In a small bowl, mix together the remaining butter and thyme leaves, the grated ginger and the mustard. Remove the chicken from the oven, arrange the potatoes around it and brush the butter mixture over the skin and on to the potatoes. Return the tin to the oven and roast for an hour, basting with the juices every so often, until the chicken is completely cooked through and the potatoes are crisp and tender.

5. Remove the chicken from the tin and leave to rest on a board for 10 minutes or so. Remove the potatoes and keep warm. Discard the celery, onions, garlic and lemon.

6. Place the roasting tin over a moderate heat and add the flour. Cook, stirring, for 1 minute, then gradually pour in the chicken stock, continuing to stir. Bring the stock up to the boil and simmer for 3–4 minutes, until slightly thickened. Strain and serve alongside the chicken and potatoes, with a handful of butter lettuce, if wished.

GINGER & COCONUT CLAYPOT CHICKEN

*DAIRY-FREE *GLUTEN-FREE

This warming dish is based on a classic Vietnamese recipe. Simple to prepare and ready in 30 minutes, it makes for a wonderful, quick alternative to a stew.

Serves 4

1 tablespoon sunflower oil
1 large onion, finely sliced
2 teaspoons palm sugar
   (finely ground if in large
   crystals)
300ml coconut water
2–3cm piece of ginger, peeled
   and finely grated
8 skinless chicken thigh fillets
1 bird's eye chilli, sliced
1–2 teaspoons fish sauce
Large pinch of ground black
   pepper
200g pak choi, sliced in half
   lengthways
Steamed rice, to serve
4 spring onions, sliced

1. Heat the oil in a large pan then add the onion and cook over a low–medium heat for 6–8 minutes, until softened and golden.

2. Whilst the onions are cooking, sprinkle the palm sugar into a separate heavy-based frying pan in an even layer. Place over a low–medium heat and allow to dissolve. As soon as the sugar is a rich golden colour, add the coconut water and turn off the heat.

3. Add the ginger to the softened onions, give it a good stir and then add the chicken.

Pour the caramel–coconut mixture into the pan and add the chilli, fish sauce and pepper. Bring to the boil then lower the heat and simmer gently for 25–30 minutes, or until the chicken is tender and cooked through.

4. Remove the chicken from the pan and set aside to rest. Add the pak choi to the pan and simmer for 2–3 minutes, until just wilted.

5. Serve the chicken over steamed rice, sprinkled with the spring onions.

CHICKEN TAGINE WITH GREEN OLIVES

*DAIRY-FREE *GLUTEN-FREE

This vibrant and aromatic tagine is so easy to prepare, and by slowly cooking the chicken, vegetables and spices, you allow the ingredients to do all of the hard work for you.

Serves 4

1 teaspoon olive oil
8 free-range chicken thighs (skin on and bone in)
2 carrots, peeled and roughly sliced into 1–2cm thick pieces
1 large onion, finely sliced
4 garlic cloves, crushed
2–3cm piece of ginger, peeled and finely grated
1½ teaspoons ground cumin
1 cinnamon stick
1 teaspoon ground turmeric
A pinch of saffron ground and soaked in 1 tablespoon warm water
12 plump green olives, such as Nocellara del Belice
350ml chicken stock
2 small preserved lemons
A handful of roughly chopped coriander, to serve
Freshly steamed couscous, to serve (optional)

1. Preheat oven to 160°C/ 140° C fan/gas mark 3.

2. Heat the oil in a large casserole dish and fry the chicken for about 5 minutes, turning occasionally, until lightly golden. Remove the chicken, set aside on a plate and drain off all but about 2 teaspoons of oil from the pan. Add the carrots, onion, garlic, ginger, cumin, cinnamon, turmeric and saffron and its soaking water to the pan. Fry for 3–4 minutes, stirring regularly, then add the olives and the stock.

3. Quarter the preserved lemons and add the roughly chopped flesh of one and the finely sliced rind of both to the pan. Return the chicken to the pan, bring up to a simmer, then cover and transfer to the oven for 50–60 minutes, until the chicken is cooked through and tender.

4. Sprinkle over the coriander and serve the tagine on its own or with freshly steamed couscous.

You can also cook this dish in a slow cooker: set it on low and cook for 4–5 hours.

DUCK SATAY *DAIRY-FREE

Making your own satay is surprisingly easy, and perfect for entertaining. Mini duck fillets require minimal cooking and result in wonderfully tender and flavoursome skewers.

Serves 4

350g mini duck fillets
1 red onion, finely sliced
1 cucumber, peeled, deseeded
  and roughly sliced

For the marinade
1 tablespoon sunflower oil
1 stalk of lemongrass, white
  part finely chopped
2 shallots, finely diced
2 garlic cloves, crushed
2–3cm piece of ginger, peeled
  and grated
5cm piece of turmeric, peeled
  and grated
1 teaspoon ground coriander
1 teaspoon chilli powder
1 teaspoon flaky sea salt
2 teaspoons light brown sugar

For the peanut sauce
1 teaspoon sunflower oil
1 shallot, finely chopped
2 garlic cloves, crushed
1 red chilli, finely chopped
1 stalk of lemongrass, white
  parts finely chopped
2–3cm piece of ginger, peeled
6 tablespoons good-quality
  crunchy peanut butter
1 tablespoon dark soy sauce
Juice of ½ lime
1 teaspoon light brown sugar

1. To make the marinade, pour the oil into a container and add the duck. Sprinkle over the remaining marinade ingredients and give everything a good stir to coat the duck. Cover and refrigerate for a minimum of 30 minutes or overnight.

2. For the peanut sauce, heat the oil in a frying pan over a low-medium heat. Add the shallots and fry for 2–3 minutes, then stir in the garlic, chilli, lemongrass and ginger. Fry for a further 2–3 minutes, until softened and fragrant. Stir through the peanut butter, soy, lime juice and sugar, along with 50ml of water. Continue stirring until combined then remove from the heat.

3. Thread the duck onto skewers (two or three fillets per skewer) and heat a griddle over a high heat. Once smoking hot, griddle the skewers for 1–2 minutes each side, until golden. The duck should still be pink, so cook for a further minute if you like them well done.

4. Serve immediately with the sauce, onion and cucumber, accompanied with steamed rice if wished.

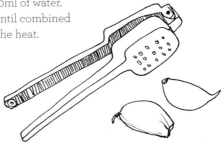

MUSSELS & FENNEL WITH WHITE WINE

GLUTEN-FREE

Rich in protein and vitamin B12, mussels are delicious, great value and surprisingly easy to cook. Teamed with lightly aniseed-flavoured fennel and white wine, this simple and flavoursome dish is ideal for a special supper or dinner with friends.

Serves 4

20g unsalted butter
1 fennel bulb, finely diced
2 shallots, finely diced
2 garlic cloves, crushed
2–3cm piece of turmeric, peeled and finely grated
1 teaspoon fennel seeds, lightly crushed
200ml dry white wine
200ml good-quality fish stock
Freshly ground black pepper
1.4kg mussels, scrubbed and de-bearded (discard any mussels with broken or cracked shells)
A handful of chopped parsley
Sourdough bread, to serve

1. Melt the butter in a very large saucepan over a low-medium heat and add the fennel and shallots. Cook gently for 10–12 minutes, until soft and translucent. Add the garlic, turmeric and fennel seeds to the pan and cook, stirring regularly, for 1–2 minutes, until fragrant.

2. Pour the white wine into the pan, increase the heat and allow to bubble for 2 minutes before pouring in the stock and a little black pepper, followed by the cleaned mussels. Cover with a lid and steam the mussels for about 5 minutes, until they have opened up. Discard any mussels that haven't opened.

3. Sprinkle over the parsley and serve immediately with good bread to mop up the juices.

COD WITH GINGER & MISO BUTTER

Nutrient- and umami-packed miso paste becomes infinitely versatile when mixed with good butter and a kick of ginger. Here it is melted over grilled cod and broccoli, but it would be equally good served on top of steak, griddled vegetables or even a baked potato. An impressive yet easy supper.

Serves 4

4 sustainable cod fillets, around 150g each
1 tablespoon mirin
1 tablespoon light soy sauce or tamari
½ teaspoon toasted sesame oil
400g tenderstem or purple sprouting broccoli
2 spring onions, finely sliced
Steamed rice, to serve (optional)

For the miso butter
40g unsalted grass-fed butter, softened
2–3cm piece of ginger, peeled and finely grated
3 tablespoons good-quality miso paste

1. To make the miso butter, mash the butter, ginger and miso paste together until smooth. Set aside in a cool place until ready to use.

2. Preheat the grill to high. Line a baking tray with foil and grease with a dot of oil. Lay the cod fillets out onto the tray. In a small bowl, whisk together the mirin and soy sauce or tamari and sprinkle over the fillets. Grill the fish for 8–10 minutes, depending on the thickness, until the fish flakes under pressure. Drizzle over the sesame seed oil.

3. Whilst the fish is cooking, steam the broccoli for 3–4 minutes, until tender but with a slight bite.

4. Serve the fish on a bed of broccoli with a knob of the miso butter on top, accompanied by rice if you like. Sprinkle with spring onions to serve.

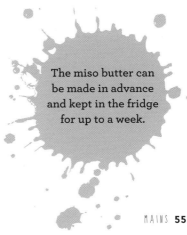

The miso butter can be made in advance and kept in the fridge for up to a week.

DRINKS, PICKLES & PRESERVES

GINGER BEER

*VEGETARIAN *DAIRY-FREE

Fiery, homemade ginger beer is perfect for a hot, summer's day. This version is made without refined sugar and, due to the fermentation process, is ever so slightly alcoholic. Not all yeast is gluten-free, so ensure you check the packet if necessary.

Makes 2–3 litres

75g fresh ginger, peeled and coarsely grated
100g soft light brown sugar, plus 1 teaspoon
150g good-quality, light runny honey
1 teaspoon cream of tartar
1 lemon, sliced
10g fresh yeast, or 4g quick yeast

1. Put the ginger, 100g sugar, honey, cream of tartar and lemon in a large stockpot or pan and pour over 2 litres of water. Bring the mixture to the boil and turn off the heat. Allow the mixture to cool to lukewarm. Mash the yeast and the teaspoon of sugar with a fork and add to the mixture. Give everything a good stir and cover the pot. Leave overnight in a cool place.

2. The next day, skim off any debris from the top of the ginger beer and strain into a large jug. Use a funnel to pour the ginger beer into sterilised bottles (see page 9), filling them no more than three quarters full as it will continue to ferment and expand in the fridge, then secure with a

cap. Release the caps every so often to release the gases and set aside in a cool, dark place.

3. The ginger beer will be ready to drink after 2 days, at which point it should be refrigerated and consumed within a week. Take care when opening the bottles and discard any beer that smells overly yeasty.

HONEY, MINT & GINGER KVASS

*VEGETARIAN *DAIRY-FREE

A traditional Slavic and Baltic fermented tonic, gut-friendly kvass is made of a base of toasted rye bread, giving it a delicious, wheaty taste. Here it is flavoured with honey, ginger and mint to add a refreshing lightness.

Makes 3 litres

400g good-quality rye bread, sliced
40g coarsely grated ginger
25g mint leaves
10g fresh bakers yeast, or 4g quick yeast
150ml good-quality runny honey
20g raisins and/or sultanas

1. Preheat the oven to 120°C/ 100°C fan/gas mark ½.

2. Lay the bread out onto baking trays and dry in the oven for about 30 minutes, until the bread is brittle and breaks easily. Put the bread in a large mixing bowl and pour over enough boiling water to cover (approximately 1 litre). Allow the water to cool before covering the bowl. Set aside in a cool, dark place overnight.

3. The following day, strain the liquid into a large container and add the ginger, mint and enough boiling water to make the mixture up to 3 litres. Allow the mixture to cool to lukewarm.

4. Mash the yeast with a teaspoon of the honey and stir into the strained liquid, along with the remaining honey. Cover the ferment and set aside for 4–6 hours, until you can see light bubbles on the surface of the mixture.

5. Skim the bubbles off then strain the kvass into a jug and use a funnel to pour into sterilised bottles (see page 9), filling them no more than three quarters full as the kvass will continue to ferment and expand in the fridge. Drop a teaspoon of raisins and/or sultanas into each bottle and refrigerate for 2 days before drinking.

6. The kvass can be kept for up to a month but be sure to open the bottles every few days to release the gases – and avoid an explosion!

BALINESE JAMU

*VEGETARIAN *GLUTEN-FREE *DAIRY-FREE

This Balinese medicinal tonic is traditionally enjoyed first thing in the morning and has been used in Bali for generations as a natural remedy to improve circulation, boost the immune system and reduce inflammation.
It can be made in larger batches and stored in the fridge for up to 2 days.

Serves 2

10cm piece of turmeric, peeled and roughly chopped
5cm piece of ginger, peeled and roughly chopped
1 stalk of lemongrass, tough outer leaves discarded, white part finely sliced
4 black peppercorns
2 cardamom pods
600ml filtered water
Juice of 1 lime
1 tablespoon good-quality honey

1. In a pestle and mortar, or food processor, combine the turmeric, ginger, lemongrass, peppercorns, cardamom and 100ml of the water until the mixture resembles a coarse purée.

2. Scoop the purée into a saucepan and pour in the remaining 500ml of water. Bring to the boil, lower the heat and simmer for 15–20 minutes, stirring occasionally.

3. Remove from the heat, strain and add the lime juice and honey.

4. The jamu can be drunk immediately or cooled and refrigerated.

TURMERIC &
CITRUS TONIC
*VEGETARIAN *GLUTEN-FREE *DAIRY-FREE

This light and refreshing tonic will keep you hydrated whilst providing a great hit of vitamins and minerals.

Serves 2

5cm piece of turmeric, peeled and finely grated
Juice of 1 red grapefruit
Juice of 1 orange
300ml sparkling water
Ice cubes, to serve
Slices of orange, to serve
2 sprigs of mint, to serve (optional)

1. Simply stir together the turmeric, grapefruit juice and orange juice, strain and top with the sparkling water.

2. Serve with ice cubes and orange slices, and a sprig of mint, if wished.

GOLDEN LASSI
*VEGETARIAN *GLUTEN-FREE

Sweet, slightly sharp and utterly refreshing, this classic drink from the Indian subcontinent is given an aromatic and anti-inflammatory boost with turmeric. Enjoy for breakfast, dessert or alongside a curry.

Serves 2

2 cardamom pods
1 teaspoon ground turmeric
Flesh from 1 large, very ripe mango or two smaller ones (Alphonso, if possible)
A handful of ice cubes
200g good-quality natural yogurt
A few tablespoons of cold water (optional)
A squeeze of lime juice (optional)

1. Bash the cardamom pods with the back of a knife and put the seeds in a blender, along with the turmeric, mango, ice cubes and yogurt. Blend until smooth. If the lassi is a little bit thick for your liking, add water to taste, but not so much that it will affect the taste.

2. Serve immediately, with a little lime juice, if liked.

GOLDEN CHAI LATTE

*VEGETARIAN *GLUTEN-FREE *DAIRY-FREE

This soothing drink is packed full of anti-inflammatory turmeric and ginger and health-giving spices. Using almond milk makes it dairy-free, but substitute with any other sugar-free milk alternative or organic cow's milk. Sweeten with good-quality honey for a comforting treat.

Serves 2

500ml organic, sugar-free almond milk (I like Rude Health)
5cm piece of turmeric, peeled and finely grated
1cm piece of ginger, peeled and finely grated
1 cardamom pod, lightly crushed
1 cinnamon stick
2 black peppercorns
1–2 teaspoons honey, to taste

1. Pour the almond milk into a pan and add the turmeric, ginger, cardamom, cinnamon and peppercorns. Place over a gentle heat and bring to a simmer. Remove from the heat, give the mixture a good stir and leave to infuse for 15 minutes.

2. Strain the milk and pour back into the pan. Place over the heat again and stir through the honey. Use a wire whisk or immersion milk frother to blend the milk and create a rich foam. Serve warm.

GINGER & TURMERIC SHOT

*VEGETARIAN *GLUTEN-FREE *DAIRY-FREE

Try having one of these shots first thing in the morning for an immune-system and anti-inflammatory hit.

Makes 2 shots

10cm piece of turmeric, peeled
5cm piece of ginger, peeled
Juice of 1 orange
A handful of ice cubes, to serve (optional)

1. Put all the ingredients through a juicer.

2. Serve immediately as a shot, or with plenty of ice for a longer drink.

GOLDEN SAUERKRAUT WITH JUNIPER

*VEGETARIAN *GLUTEN-FREE *DAIRY-FREE

Fermented cabbage may not sound like the most glamorous of foods but this delicious, lightly sour recipe is worth the effort and will make a gut-friendly addition to many meals. Try it heaped on salad or alongside grilled meat or vegetables.

Makes 2 x 450ml jars

1kg firm white cabbage, core and tough outer leaves removed, finely shredded
3 tablespoons flaky sea salt
½ teaspoon peppercorns
2–3cm piece of turmeric, peeled and thinly sliced
2 teaspoons juniper berries

1. Because sauerkraut is fermented, everything that comes into contact with it at the preparation stage needs to be scrupulously clean. Thoroughly wash a large mixing bowl, a container large enough to fit the sauerkraut, and any utensils, such as a knife and chopping board, that will come into contact with the cabbage.

2 Tip the cabbage into a large bowl, sprinkle over the salt and set aside for 15 minutes to soften.

3. Massage the cabbage vigorously with your hands for about 10 minutes, until the cabbage has softened and there is plenty of liquid. Mix in the peppercorns, turmeric and juniper berries and stir to combine. Transfer the sauerkraut to a container and use the back of a very clean spoon to press the cabbage down so that it is compact. Cover the cabbage mix tightly with a sheet of clingfilm and then weigh down with a plate. Cover the container with its lid or in clingfilm and leave in a cool dark place.

4. Check the sauerkraut every day or so, pressing down with the back of a clean spoon again to release any bubbles and skimming off any scum that may have formed on the surface. The sauerkraut will be ready to eat after 5 days but you can keep fermenting it for up to 2 weeks, until it is to your liking.

5. Once the sauerkraut is of the desired sourness, sterilise two jars (see page 9) and carefully spoon in the sauerkraut, using a clean spoon. Transfer to the fridge, where it will keep for up to 6 months.

ACHAR *VEGETARIAN *GLUTEN-FREE *DAIRY-FREE

This classic Nyonya pickle offers a sweet, sour and crunchy foil to rich Southeast Asian food. It's a great source of dietary fibre and full of vitamins A and C, along with a healthy dose of probiotics from the pickling process. Enjoy either before dinner or as a side dish.

Makes 2 x 500ml jars

4 shallots, peeled and roughly chopped
4 red chillies, chopped
1 teaspoon chilli flakes
5cm piece of turmeric, peeled and roughly chopped
4 garlic cloves
2–3cm piece of ginger, peeled and roughly chopped
2 tablespoons vegetable oil
70g soft light brown sugar
100ml rice vinegar
1 tablespoon flaky sea salt
50g roasted salted peanuts, finely chopped
1 tablespoon sesame seeds, toasted
200g pineapple, peeled, cored and cut into 2cm pieces

For the vegetables
350g cucumber, deseeded and cut into 5cm-long strips
200g white cabbage, core and tough outer leaves removed, cut into 2cm pieces
150g carrot, peeled and cut into 5cm-long strips
2 tablespoons flaky sea salt

1. Blitz the shallots, chillies, chilli flakes, turmeric, garlic and ginger in a food-processor until you have a fine paste.

2. Heat the oil in a frying pan and add the spice mixture. Cook, stirring regularly, for 3–4 minutes, until fragrant. Add the sugar, vinegar and salt and stir until the sugar has dissolved. Set aside to cool slightly.

3. Meanwhile, put the cucumber, cabbage and carrot in a colander and sprinkle over the salt. Leave the vegetables to sit for 30 minutes, then rinse off the brine. Wrap the vegetables in a piece of muslin or a tea-towel and squeeze out any excess liquid.

4. Mix the peanuts and sesame seeds into the spice paste before stirring through the vegetables and pineapple.

5. Transfer the achar to sterilised jars (see page 9). Stored in the fridge, it will keep for up to a month.

PLUM & GINGER COMPOTE

*VEGETARIAN *GLUTEN-FREE *DAIRY-FREE

This quick and simple compote is so versatile; try a dollop on yogurt, mixed with granola for breakfast or with ice cream for a simple dessert.

Serves 8–10

750g plums, stones removed
and cut into quarters
50ml good-quality runny
honey or maple syrup
2–3cm piece of ginger, peeled
and finely grated
1 vanilla pod, split lengthways,
seeds scraped out with the
back of a knife

1. Tip all of the ingredients into a large, heavy-based saucepan and add 50ml water. Bring the mixture to the boil, stirring all the while, and once boiling, lower the heat and simmer very gently for 5–6 minutes, until the plums have begun to soften but are still holding their shape.

2. Allow to cool and then refrigerate. The compote can be kept in the fridge for up to 3 days or in the freezer for up to 3 months.

Use any seasonal soft fruit instead of plums such as berries, currants, peaches, apricots or figs.

TOMATO & GINGER CHUTNEY *VEGETARIAN *GLUTEN-FREE *DAIRY-FREE

This chutney is ideal for using up a glut of overripe tomatoes. As good with cheese and cold meats as it is with roasted vegetables, or even stirred through yogurt to make a lively dip.

Makes 5 x 250ml jars

2 large red onions, finely sliced

1kg overripe tomatoes, roughly chopped

3 garlic cloves, crushed

5cm piece of ginger, peeled and coarsely grated

125g soft light brown sugar

100ml apple cider vinegar

1½ teaspoons yellow mustard seeds

¼ teaspoon crushed chilli flakes

1. Tip all of the ingredients into a very large, heavy-based saucepan and bring up to simmering point, stirring all the while. When the mixture is simmering, lower the heat and let the chutney bubble away very gently for 1 hour, stirring every now and then. The chutney is ready when most of the liquid has been absorbed and it is of a fairly thick, jammy consistency.

2. Leave to cool slightly before spooning into hot, sterilised jars (see page 9). Secure with a vinegar-proof lid and set aside in a cool, dark place for 6 weeks to allow the flavours to develop before opening. Once opened, refrigerate and consume within 2 weeks.

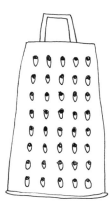

SWEET
TREATS

STONE FRUIT & TURMERIC GALETTE

*VEGETARIAN

Galettes are possibly the easiest tart that you can make and offer a great introduction into pastry making. This richly fruited tart really showcases the versatility of turmeric. Used here in the pastry, along with hazelnuts, its earthy, slightly aromatic undertones complement the stone fruits perfectly. Of course, this tart is best made when the fruits are in season, when they will be at their sweetest, most nutritious and most flavoursome.

Serves 10–12

For the pastry
275g plain flour
75g ground hazelnuts
Pinch of salt
175g cold unsalted butter, cut into small cubes
40g golden caster sugar
2 teaspoons ground turmeric
1 medium egg, separated

For the filling
600g stone fruits – any combination of peaches, nectarines, plums, apricots and cherries
40g soft light brown sugar
1½ teaspoons cornflour
1 teaspoon ground cinnamon
30g hazelnuts, roughly chopped

cont. overleaf

1. To make the pastry, tip the flour, ground hazelnuts and salt into the bowl of a food-processor and blitz until well combined. Add the butter and pulse until the mixture resembles fine breadcrumbs. Add the caster sugar and turmeric, pulse again to combine then add the egg yolk, along with 1 tablespoon of ice-cold water. Pulse until the mixture starts to come together. If it doesn't start forming a ball, add up to another tablespoon of water.

2. Tip the pastry onto a clean, lightly floured surface and shape into a disc. Wrap in clingfilm and refrigerate for 45 minutes to rest. Meanwhile, preheat the oven to 190°C/170°C fan/gas mark 5.

3. To prepare the fruit for the filling, halve and stone the cherries, stone and quarter the plums and apricots and stone and cut the peaches and nectarines into eighths. Tip the fruit into a large mixing bowl and sprinkle over the sugar, cornflour and cinnamon. Mix well to ensure that all of the fruits are well coated and set aside.

4. To assemble the tart, lay a sheet of greaseproof paper onto a work surface and place the chilled pastry in the middle.

cont. overleaf

Crème fraîche, yogurt or a
dollop of good ice cream, to
serve

Very gently roll the pastry out
into a circle measuring about
35cm, lightly flouring the pastry
as you go to stop it sticking to
the rolling pin, and pinching
back together any cracks that
may appear. At this point, you
can neaten up the edges with a
knife if you like, but remember
that this tart is supposed to
be rustic so neatness is not
imperative. Carefully lift the
paper to transfer the pastry onto
a flat baking tray.

5. Tip the fruits into the centre
of the pastry and spread them
out a little, leaving a 6cm border
all around the edge of the pastry.
Whisk the reserved egg white

until lightly frothy and brush
a little onto the pastry border.
Carefully fold the pastry up
over the fruits, again pinching
any cracks together, and brush
the pastry with more egg white.
Sprinkle over the chopped
hazelnuts and transfer to the
oven.

6. Bake the galette for 45–50
minutes, until the pastry is
golden and crisp and the fruits
are soft. Resist the temptation to
serve straight away as the filling
will be very runny. Allow the
tart to cool for 20–30 minutes
and serve in slices with crème
fraîche, yogurt or a dollop of
good ice cream.

GINGER & FIG GRANOLA
*VEGETARIAN *DAIRY-FREE

For an all-round health-boosting breakfast, try making your own granola. Rich in fibre, antioxidants and slow-release energy, this refined sugar-free granola will get your day off to the best possible start.

Makes approximately 1kg (enough for 20+ servings)

50g coconut oil
100ml honey
75ml maple syrup
3 teaspoons ground ginger
450g rolled oats (gluten-free, if necessary)
100g pecans, roughly chopped
100g pistachios, roughly chopped
75g linseeds or pumpkin seeds
2 tablespoons sesame seeds
Pinch of flaked sea salt
2 medium egg whites
150g dried figs, roughly chopped

1. Preheat the oven to 150°C/130°C fan/gas mark 2. Line two large baking trays with greaseproof paper.

2. Put the coconut oil, honey, maple syrup and ground ginger into a saucepan and heat gently until the oil has melted.

3. Put the oats, nuts, seeds and salt into a large mixing bowl and stir together. Pour over the oil mixture and give everything a good stir.

4. In another clean, dry bowl, beat the egg whites separately until lightly frothy then stir this into the granola.

5. Spread the mixture out in a thin layer onto the lined baking trays and bake for 20 minutes, then mix in the figs and return to the oven for a further 20–25 minutes, until golden and crisp.

6. Remove from the oven and allow to cool before decanting into an airtight container. This should keep the granola fresh for up to a month.

PINEAPPLE & TURMERIC PANCAKES

*VEGETARIAN

These golden pancakes are a healthy take on the American classics. This recipe has the addition of a layer of pineapple, which caramelises to delicious effect whilst cooking, making it a real treat. Serve with honey and lime juice for a weekend breakfast.

Serves 4

125g wholemeal plain flour
1½ teaspoons baking powder
1 teaspoon ground turmeric
½ teaspoon ground cinnamon
Pinch of salt
2 tablespoons coconut sugar (or soft light brown sugar)
200ml milk
1 large egg, lightly beaten
1 tablespoon coconut oil, melted, plus extra for cooking (or use melted butter or light olive oil)
1 small fresh pineapple (about 500g), peeled and flesh cut into ½ cm thick slices
60ml honey
Finely grated zest and juice of ½ lime

1. Sift the flour, baking powder, turmeric, cinnamon and a pinch of salt into a mixing bowl and stir through the sugar. Tip any flakes of bran from the flour that remain in the sieve into the bowl.

2. In a separate bowl or jug, beat together the milk, egg and coconut oil. Make a well in the centre of the dry mixture and pour in the wet ingredients. Beat with a whisk, gradually drawing the dry ingredients into the well, to make a smooth batter.

3. Place a large, non-stick pan over a low–medium heat and wipe with a little oil or butter. Drop a large tablespoon of the mixture into the pan and repeat so that you have two to three pancakes cooking at the same time – allowing for the fact that the batter will spread slightly when the pineapple is added. Blot the pineapple slices dry and lay one slice over each pancake. Cook for 2–3 minutes, until bubbles appear on the surface of each pancake and the edges are set. Carefully flip over and cook for a further 2–3 minutes, until golden. Keep warm and repeat until the mixture has been used up.

4. To serve, whisk together the honey, lime juice and zest and pour over the pancakes.

VANILLA FIGS WITH STREUSEL TOPPING
*VEGETARIAN

These simple to prepare yet delicious baked figs are as good for dessert as they are for an indulgent breakfast.

Serves 4

8 ripe figs, cut in half
1 vanilla pod, cut in half and
  seeds scraped out
Juice of 1 orange
Mascarpone or natural yogurt,
  to serve (optional)

For the streusel topping
50g wholemeal plain flour
35g cold unsalted butter, cut
  into cubes
1½ teaspoons ground ginger
20g soft light brown sugar
20g pistachios, roughly
  chopped

1. Preheat the oven to 180°C/ 160°C fan/gas mark 4.

2. Lay the figs out in an even layer in an ovenproof dish, cut side up. Stir together the vanilla seeds and orange juice and pour over the figs. Add the vanilla pod to the dish.

3. To make the streusel topping, tip the flour into a mixing bowl, add the butter and rub in until the mixture resembles large breadcrumbs and no lumps of butter remain. Stir through

the remaining ingredients and sprinkle the streusel mix over the figs.

4. Bake in the oven for 20–25 minutes, until the streusel is crisp and golden. Serve with a dollop of mascarpone or yogurt, if liked.

The streusel can also be used as an alternative to a crumble topping. Scatter over stewed fruit and bake.

WATERMELON, MINT & GINGER ICE

*VEGETARIAN *GLUTEN-FREE *DAIRY-FREE

Sweet and nutrient-rich watermelon is given a kick by a hint of spicy ginger and mellowed with a little mint in this refreshing ice. The addition of salt may seem surprising, but it really makes the flavours sing.

Makes 1.5 litres

1kg watermelon flesh
Good pinch of flaky sea salt
2 tablespoons honey
30g piece of ginger, peeled
    and very finely grated
Small handful of mint leaves
    (about 5g), finely chopped
Extra mint leaves, chopped, to
    serve (optional)

1. Place the watermelon flesh in a food-processor with the salt and honey and process until smooth. Pass through a sieve to remove the seeds before stirring through the ginger and mint until evenly dispersed.

2. Pour the mixture into a 1.5 litre capacity container and place in the freezer. Give the mixture a good stir and scrape every hour to break up the large ice crystals until the mixture is set and of a fine, icy texture. Serve with a little extra mint on top, if liked.

GINGER CHOCOLATE BISCOTTI *VEGETARIAN *GLUTEN-FREE

A healthier, gluten-free version of the Italian classic, but no less delicious. Biscotti are easy to make and perfect with a cup of coffee or to have on-hand for an afternoon treat.

Makes up to 16 biscotti

300g ground almonds
2 teaspoons arrowroot
½ teaspoon bicarbonate of soda
3 teaspoons ground ginger
Finely grated zest of 4 clementines or satsumas
75g coconut sugar
75g pistachios or blanched hazelnuts
2 medium eggs, beaten
½ tablespoon coconut oil, melted
100g dark chocolate, at least 70% cocoa solids

1. Preheat the oven to 200°C/180°C fan/gas mark 6. Line a baking tray with greaseproof or waxed paper.

2. Pour the ground almonds, arrowroot, bicarbonate of soda, ground ginger, clementine zest, coconut sugar and nuts into a large bowl and stir to combine. Add the beaten egg and briskly stir the ingredients together to form a soft, slightly stick dough.

3. Shape the dough into a log, about 30cm long and flatten slightly. Transfer to the prepared baking tray and bake for 15 minutes. Remove from the oven and set aside for 45 minutes.

4. Turn the heat of the oven down to 180°C/160°C fan/gas mark 4. Use a sharp bread knife to cut the log into 1–2cm thick slices and return to the baking tray, sliced side up. Brush a little of the oil over each biscuit and return to the oven for 10 minutes. Turn the biscotti over, brush with a little more oil and return to the oven for a further 10 minutes, until crisp and golden. Remove from the oven and transfer to a wire rack to cool.

5. Once the biscotti have cooled, melt the chocolate and dip one end of each biscuit into it. Either eat immediately or lay on a sheet of greaseproof or waxed paper until set.

CARDAMOM & TURMERIC BUNS *VEGETARIAN

These sunny-hued and aromatic buns are a healthier twist on a Swedish classic. They take a little time to make but are well worth the effort.

Makes 16 buns

For the dough

250ml whole milk
80g unsalted butter, cubed
4 tablespoons good-quality runny honey
25g fresh yeast, crumbled, or 1 teaspoon fast-action yeast
500g strong white bread flour
1 tablespoon ground turmeric
1½ teaspoons ground cardamom
½ teaspoon salt
1 medium egg, lightly beaten
A little oil, for greasing

For the filling

125g unsalted butter, softened
75g ground almonds
25g soft light brown sugar
2 teaspoons ground cardamom
Seeds from 1 vanilla pod
4 tablespoons good-quality runny honey
1 egg, for brushing

1. Heat the milk until it is just beginning to bubble at the edges, then add the butter. Swirl the pan to melt the butter then leave to cool until lukewarm (using cold butter will speed up this process).

2. Add the honey and yeast, then stir until dissolved. Set aside for 10–15 minutes until foamy.

3. Sift the flour, turmeric, cardamom and salt into a large bowl or a free standing mixer. Make a well in the centre and pour in the milk and egg. Use a wooden spoon or dough hook to mix to a soft dough. Knead for 5–10 minutes, either in the mixer or by hand, until smooth and elastic, and springing back to the touch. Clean the bowl, grease with the oil and return the dough, turning it over a couple of times to coat. Cover with clingfilm, then set aside until doubled in size – about 2 hours.

4. Meanwhile, beat together the butter, almonds, sugar, cardamom, vanilla and honey

until smooth and spreadable.

5. Knead the dough for another minute on a lightly floured surface, then roll out to a rectangle about 1cm thick. Spread evenly with the filling, then roll up tightly from the longest edge. With a sharp knife, cut into 16 even slices and divide between two baking trays lined with greaseproof paper, leaving gaps of about 2cm. Cover with lightly oiled clingfilm and leave for 1 hour, until almost doubled in size and not springing back. Carefully brush any exposed dough with the beaten egg.

6. Whilst the dough is rising, preheat the oven to 190°C/170°C fan/gas mark 5.

7. Bake the buns for 10 minutes, then cover with greaseproof paper and bake for a further 10 minutes, until golden.

8. Remove from the oven and transfer to a wire rack to cool slightly before serving.

GRAPEFRUIT, ALMOND & TURMERIC CAKE

*VEGETARIAN *GLUTEN-FREE *DAIRY-FREE

This vibrantly coloured, zesty cake is free of refined sugar, which allows the flavours of the grapefruit to shine through.

Cuts into 12 slices

200g ground almonds
125g polenta
125g golden caster sugar
2 teaspoons ground turmeric
1½ teaspoons gluten-free baking powder
110ml fruity olive oil
4 tablespoons good-quality runny honey
3 large eggs
Finely grated zest of 2 red grapefruit and juice of 1
Pinch of salt

1. Preheat the oven to 180°C/160°C fan/gas mark 4. Lightly grease a 20cm-diameter round cake tin and line the base with greaseproof or waxed paper.

2. Pour all of the ingredients into a large mixing bowl and use an electric hand whisk to beat until smooth. You can also do this in a food-processor.

3. Pour the mixture into the prepared tin and bake for 50 minutes to an hour, until the cake is golden, well risen and a skewer inserted into the centre comes out clean.

4. Leave to cool in the tin for 20 minutes, before turning out onto a wire rack to cool completely.

This cake is delicious served warm with a dollop of crème fraîche and a sprig of thyme.

INDEX

ACKNOWLEDGEMENTS

I would firstly like to thank all at Kyle Books for inviting me to write a second book for *The Goodness Of* series; It's such an honour to write for a publishing company whose books I have always loved buying and cooking from.

I would like to thank Claire Rogers for her help and guidance at the beginning of this project, and then Hannah Coughlin for taking on the mantle, steering me through the recipe writing process and organising the shoot days – it has been such a pleasure to work with you both. I'd also like to thank Fiona Rose for her eagle-eyed proofreading and Helen Bratby for her brilliant and thoughtful design.

Cookbooks should not only serve as instructive manuals, but be feasts for the eyes to inspire the reader. I'd like to thank Faith Mason for her beautiful images and creativity and Jacqui Melville of Ginger Whisk for her gorgeous props that complemented the food so well. Thanks to Nicola Roberts, Emma Laws and Elayna Rudolphy for their help on shoots and notes on recipes. Also to the wonderful Mrs. Mahon who helped me with the recipe testing.

I'd like to extend special thanks for my dear friend Jenni Desmond who has lent her lovely illustrations to all of the books in this series. They add such fun and charm to the book and I love that we have joint projects.

Finally, I'd like to thank Bob for being my most honest and supportive taste-tester. It's a tough job, having to work your way through endless plates of food but you handle it admirably. I wrote this book whilst on a grown-up gap year and so I'd like to give my final thanks to my sister, Jess, and Will, for putting up with me taking over their spare room and kitchen; I hope that the titbits have made up for it.

For my dear and much missed grandmother, 'Bobbus.'

An Hachette UK Company
www.hachette.co.uk

First published in Great Britain in 2018
by Kyle Books, an imprint of Kyle
Cathie Ltd
Carmelite House, 50 Victoria Embankment
London EC4Y 0DZ
www.kylebooks.co.uk

10 9 8 7 6 5 4 3 2

ISBN 978 0 85783 462 1

Distributed in the US by Hachette Book
Group, 1290 Avenue of the Americas,
4th and 5th Floors, New York, NY 10104

Distributed in Canada by Canadian Manda
Group, 664 Annette St., Toronto, Ontario,
Canada M6S 2C8

Project Editor: Hannah Coughlin
Copy Editor: Anne McDowall
Designer: Helen Bratby
Photographer: Faith Mason
Illustrator: Jenni Desmond
Food Stylist: Emily Jonzen
Prop Stylist: Ginger Whisk
Production: Nic Jones and Gemma John

A Cataloguing in Publication record
for this title is available from the British
Library.

Printed and bound in China

* Note: all eggs are free-range